W9-AZU-474

Tell Me Why

WHY?

Spiders Weave Webs

Katie Marsico

Published in the United States of America by Cherry Lake Publishing
Ann Arbor, Michigan
www.cherrylakepublishing.com

Content Adviser: Todd A. Blackledge, Professor of Biology at the University of Akron
Reading Adviser: Marla Conn, ReadAbility, Inc

Photo Credits: © val r/Shutterstock Images, cover, 1, 13; © LFRabanedo/Shutterstock Images, cover, 1, 5;
© EcoPrint/Shutterstock Images, 7; © BlueRingMedia/Shutterstock Images, 9; © Robyn Butler/Shutterstock
Images, 11; © Cathy Keifer/Shutterstock Images, 15; © Dmitrijs Mihejevs/Shutterstock Images, cover, 1, 17;
© Di Studio/Shutterstock Images, 19; © alybaba/Shutterstock Images, 21

Library of Congress Cataloging-in-Publication Data

Marsico, Katie, 1980-author.
  Spiders weave webs / by Katie Marsico.
     pages cm.—(Tell me why)
  Audience: Ages 6–10
  Audience: K to grade 3
  Includes bibliographical references and index.
  ISBN 978-1-63362-617-1 (hardcover)—ISBN 978-1-63362-707-9 (pbk.)—ISBN 978-1-63362-797-0 (pdf)—
ISBN 978-1-63362-887-8 (ebook)
  1. Spider webs—Juvenile literature. 2. Spiders—Juvenile literature. I. Title. II. Series: Tell me why?
(Cherry Lake Publishing)

QL458.4.M357 2016
595.4'4—dc23

                                        2015005652

Cherry Lake Publishing would like to acknowledge the work of the Partnership for 21st Century Skills.
Please visit *www.p21.org* for more information.

Printed in the United States of America
Corporate Graphics

Table of Contents

What a Web!

Eek! Spider! Bella was startled when she spied an eight-legged visitor moving along her basement wall. She watched as it scurried into a delicate white web in the corner of the ceiling.

Mom told her that the spider probably spun the web. Bella was curious exactly how it managed to do this. Just as importantly, she wondered *why* the spider spun the web in the first place!

LOOK!

This cellar spider is also known as a daddy longlegs spider. How do you think it got its name? Have you ever seen one before?

People often find spiders in their basements, but most of them are harmless.

Mom explained that many spiders make webs to trap **prey**. They are predators and kill other animals for food. Since spiders are carnivorous, their diet is made up of the meat of these animals.

Most **species** feed on insects such as flies, moths, roaches, earwigs, and mosquitoes. But some, such as golden orb-weaving spiders, eat larger prey. Once in awhile, their webs catch small birds and bats.

These spiders have caught a moth.

Spiders are **arachnids**, not insects. There are several important differences between these two **classes** of animals. An arachnid's body is made up of two main divisions. Meanwhile, an insect's body has three divisions.

Also, insects have three pairs of legs, while arachnids have four. Finally, unlike insects, arachnids lack **antennae**. Other examples of arachnids include mites, scorpions, and ticks.

Spider Anatomy

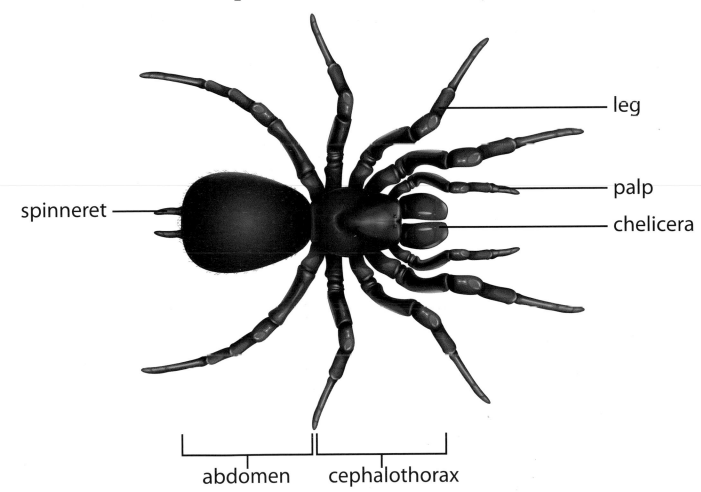

leg

palp

chelicera

spinneret

abdomen   cephalothorax

Insects have six legs, but spiders have eight.

Web-Building Basics

Bella and her mom used a magnifying glass to take a closer look at the web. How did the spider manage to spin all those **spiraled** threads? Mom explained that it has special **glands** in its abdomen, or hind section. These glands produce **proteins** that are forced through **organs** called spinnerets.

Before the proteins reach the openings of the spinnerets, they're stretched and joined together. Eventually the spinnerets combine the proteins into long threads of silk.

This spider is hard at work, weaving a web.

A spider often starts building a web by releasing a single thread into the air. It then waits for the free end of the thread to hook onto a nearby object. From this starting point, it uses more thread to create even more anchors.

Soon, the spider forms a **frame** for the web. It then spins threads that stretch between the frame and points within the area it surrounds. Some of the threads are smooth, while others are sticky.

Are you able to guess why some of the threads in a spider web need to be sticky?

The strands of a spiderweb are usually too thin to see, but this one has dewdrops covering it.

13

A Sticky Situation

Bella found herself stuck on the word *sticky*. Suddenly, she began to understand how spiders use their webs to trap prey! Insects and other small animals become caught in the sticky threads. Afterward, they struggle to free themselves.

This motion causes the web to **vibrate**. The spider senses these vibrations. They provide information about where the prey is located within the web.

But now Bella was curious about something else. She wondered how spiders avoid getting trapped along with their prey!

How can spiders spin both sticky and smooth silk? Ask an arachnologist! (That's a spider expert.)

This insect has been trapped in the sticky web.

Scientists believe there are a few answers to Bella's question. The threads that are sticky are dotted with a glue-like substance. It's likely that spiders try to avoid areas where this substance is present.

Some spiders also have extra claws on their feet. This helps them grip, or grab onto, the threads they spin. Extra claws make it easier for spiders to move carefully and quickly through the tangles of their web.

The texture of spiders' legs allows them to walk across their webs without getting stuck.

Spectacular Spider Silk

After talking to Mom, Bella found spiders far more interesting than frightening. Mom told her that other people feel the same way about these arachnids and their webs. Scientists are busily studying human uses for spider silk. They're exploring possibilities that range from bandages to seat belts. Some scientists have even suggested that spider silk would be helpful in making parachutes and bulletproof clothing.

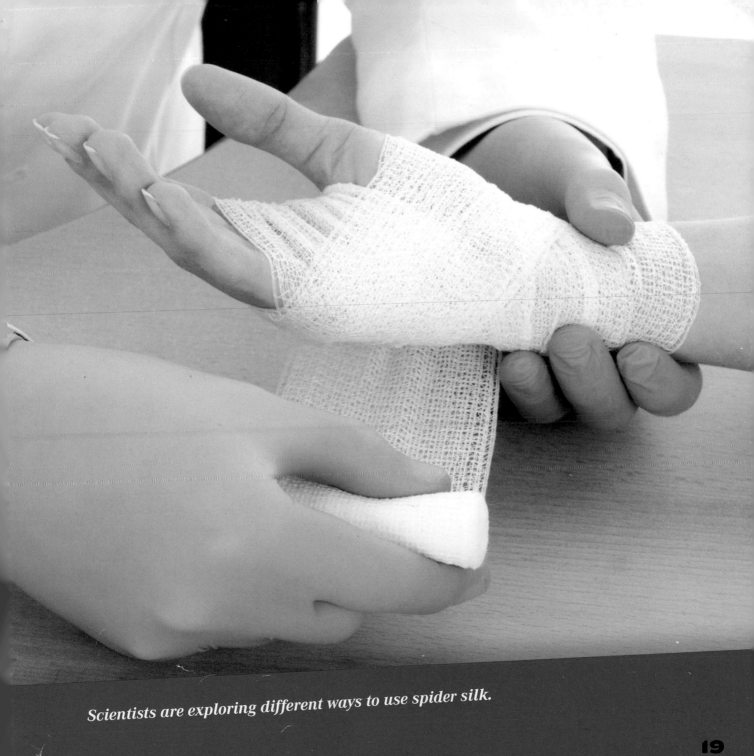

Scientists are exploring different ways to use spider silk.

Bella asked Mom if the spider was dangerous. Mom said that only about forty species out of thousands are known to bite humans. The one they saw was a cellar spider. Luckily, this species is harmless.

Bella decided to leave the spider web in her basement alone. She came to the conclusion that their eight-legged guest was performing an important job for her family. Thanks to the spider and its web, it would be easier to keep their home insect-free!

If you see a spider, the best thing to do is leave it alone.

Think About It!

Not all spiders build webs, but they still need to find and kill food. What other ways do you think these spiders capture their next meal? Go online to find out.

Think about where you've seen spider webs around your home or yard. What made you notice the webs in the first place? Are they located in light or dark areas? Damp or dry? Have you ever observed prey trapped in the silk threads? Think about whether you see more or fewer insects in areas with spider webs. What does this tell you?

Glossary

antennae (an-TEN-ee) thin, sensitive organs on the head of an insect that it uses to feel and touch its surrounding environment

arachnids (uh-RAK-nuhdz) animals such as spiders that lack a backbone and antennae and that have two main body divisions and four pairs of legs

classes (KLAS-uhz) categories that group different orders of animals together according to traits that they share

frame (FRAYM) a structure that surrounds or supports an inner area or space

glands (GLANDZ) organs in the body that produce natural chemical substances

organs (OR-guhnz) body parts that perform a specific job

prey (PRAY) animals killed by other animals for food

proteins (PROH-teenz) substances made by the body to support health and various body processes

species (SPEE-sheez) one type, or kind, of plant or animal

spiraled (SPYE-ruhld) winding in a continuous curve around a fixed point

vibrate (vye-BRAYTE) to shake quickly or move with rapid, back-and-forth motions

Find Out More

Books:

Ripley's Believe It or Not! *Spiders and Scary Creepy Crawlies*. Orlando, FL: Ripley Publishing, 2014.

Salzmann, Mary Elizabeth. *Home Sweet Web*. Minneapolis: ABDO Publishing Company, 2012.

Web Sites:

BioKIDS—Webs and Cocoons
www.biokids.umich.edu/guides/tracks_and_sign/build/webs/
Learn additional facts about the wide variety of webs that spiders spin.

Kids Konnect—Spiders
https://kidskonnect.com/animals/spider/
Find out more interesting information about these amazing arachnids.

Index

About the Author

Katie Marsico is the author of more than 200 children's books. She lives in a suburb of Chicago, Illinois, with her husband and children.